PLASTICS

© Aladdin Books Ltd 1987

Designed and produced by
Aladdin Books Ltd
70 Old Compton Street
London W1

First published in
Great Britain in 1987 by
Franklin Watts
12a Golden Square
London W1

ISBN 0 86313 549 8

Printed in Belgium

Design   David West
                Children's Book Design

Editor   Margaret Fagan

Researcher   Cecilia Weston-Baker

Illustrators   Louise Nevett
                Simon Bishop

Consultant   Ian Mercer
                Geological Museum, London

CONTENTS

Photographic Credits:
Cover and pages 23 and
24: Robert Harding; title
page and page 4-5: Tony
Stone Associates; pages 9
and 21: Shell
Photographic; pages 15,
17 and 19: Photosource;
page 18: Paul Brierley.

PLASTICS

Kathryn Whyman

GLOUCESTER PRESS
London · New York · Toronto · Sydney

WHAT IS A PLASTIC?

Plastics are everywhere! As you read this book perhaps you are sitting on a plastic chair, leaning on a plastic-coated table or wearing plastic shoes. There are many different types of plastic. For example, the plastic of a washing-up bowl is quite different from the plastic cups in a drinks machine. So what makes something a plastic? Any man-made material which can be moulded into any shape is a plastic. This feature is one of the reasons why plastics are so useful.

Plastics are mass produced in factories

There are other reasons why plastics play an important part in our lives. They are light and relatively cheap. They can be produced in different colours. Heat and electricity do not travel through them easily – they are good "insulators". Unlike metals and wood, they do not rust or rot. But plastics do have some disadvantages too. They are not as strong as many metals and they melt at high temperatures – sometimes giving off poisonous fumes.

WHERE DO PLASTICS COME FROM?

Plastics can be made from chemicals found in coal, gas or crude oil. At the moment most plastic is made from crude oil as this is cheaper. But as the world's reserves of crude oil begin to run out coal may be used instead. Crude oil is a liquid found below the surface of the earth. It is not a single substance. It is a mixture of many chemicals. Some of these chemicals can be used to make plastics.

The first stage in making plastics is to pipe the crude oil to an oil refinery. At the refinery the oil is separated into its different chemicals. Many are used as fuels but some, especially naphtha, are further processed to make plastics.

The refinery where thousands of tonnes of oil are processed

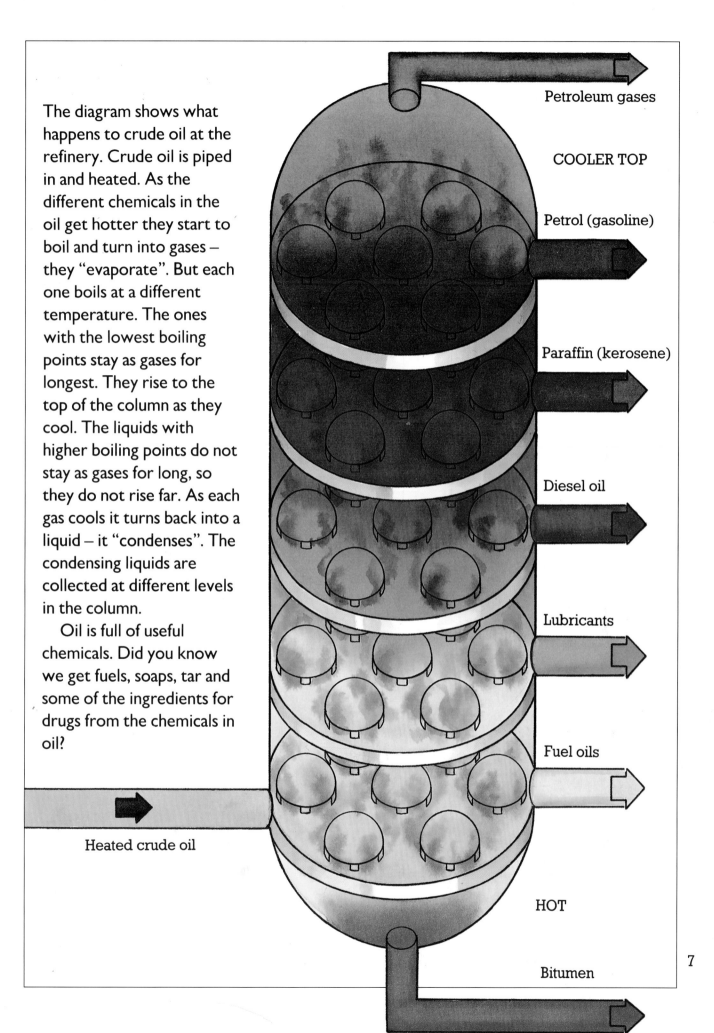

The diagram shows what happens to crude oil at the refinery. Crude oil is piped in and heated. As the different chemicals in the oil get hotter they start to boil and turn into gases – they "evaporate". But each one boils at a different temperature. The ones with the lowest boiling points stay as gases for longest. They rise to the top of the column as they cool. The liquids with higher boiling points do not stay as gases for long, so they do not rise far. As each gas cools it turns back into a liquid – it "condenses". The condensing liquids are collected at different levels in the column.

Oil is full of useful chemicals. Did you know we get fuels, soaps, tar and some of the ingredients for drugs from the chemicals in oil?

Petroleum gases

COOLER TOP

Petrol (gasoline)

Paraffin (kerosene)

Diesel oil

Lubricants

Fuel oils

Heated crude oil

HOT

Bitumen

7

HOW ARE PLASTICS MADE?

Naphtha is a light sort of oil. Even though it is one of the chemicals in oil it is not a pure substance. It can be separated into yet more chemicals in a process called "cracking". One of the pure chemicals obtained during cracking is "ethene". Ethene is one of the most useful chemicals for making plastics. It is usually a colourless, inflammable gas. Like all substances, ethene is made up of tiny particles called "molecules". These molecules are separate in the gas but in special circumstances they can be joined together in chains, rather like a long row of beads. When this happens the plastic "polythene" is formed – one of the world's most widely used plastics.

Ethene molecules

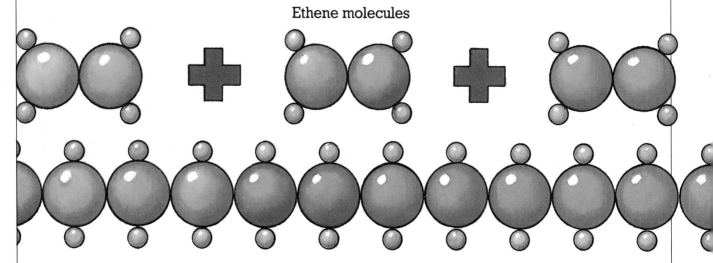

Polythene

Each molecule of ethene is made up of two atoms of carbon and four of hydrogen. The top part of the diagram shows three of these molecules. They are separate as they would be in ethene gas. But if another chemical, known as a "catalyst" is added, these molecules join together to form a long chain. The process of joining molecules in this way is called "polymerisation" and the chain itself is called a "polymer". Polythene gets its name from "poly" meaning many, and ethene. Other plastics can be made in a similar way.

Most plastics are made from oil – the inset shows polystyrene used for packaging

TYPES OF PLASTIC

Although there are many different plastics, they can all be divided into just two groups. These are the "thermoplastics" and the "thermosetting plastics". Polystyrene, polyvinyl chloride (PVC) and polythene were the first thermoplastics to be developed and they are still widely used. More recently thermoplastics, such as Nylon, Perspex and Orlon have been produced.

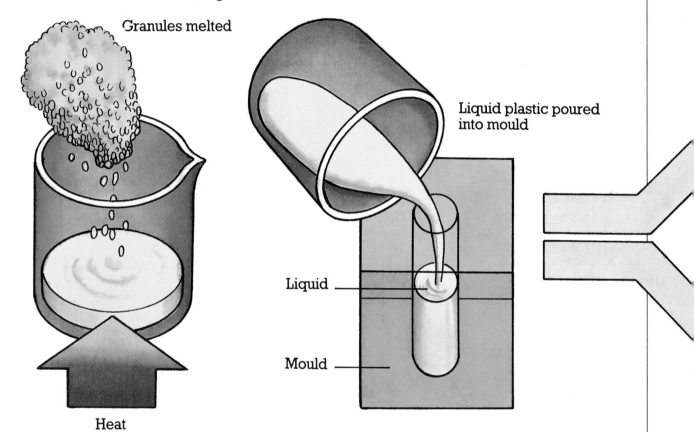

Granules melted

Liquid plastic poured into mould

Liquid

Mould

Heat

When plastics are first made they are either in the form of a thick liquid or – more usually – solid granules. This material is called "raw plastic" as it is not yet shaped into a finished article. The granules are tipped into a container and heated until they melt. They may contain a colouring dye.

The liquid plastic is then poured into a mould. There are several types of mould but the simplest is just a hollow piece of metal. The shape inside it is exactly the same shape as the finished article will be. Up until this point the thermoplastics and the thermosetting plastics are treated in the same way.

The common feature of thermoplastics is that they all melt when heated to high enough temperatures and set solid again as they cool. This means they can be re-used. But thermosetting plastics do not have this property. They are resistant to much higher temperatures. For this reason they are often used to make saucepan handles and ashtrays. The first plastic ever made was a thermosetting plastic called Bakelite after its inventor Leo Baekeland.

THERMOSETTING

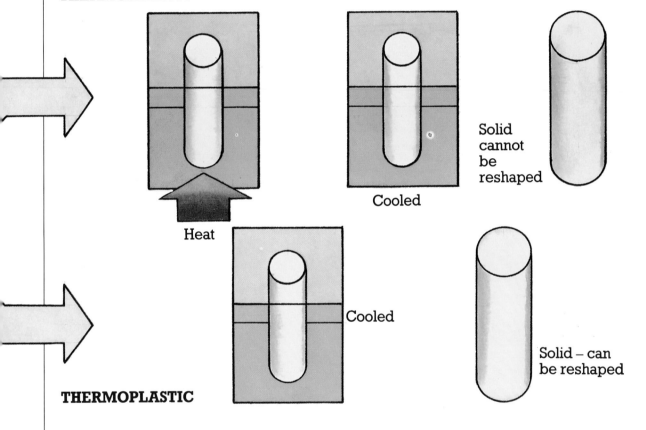

THERMOPLASTIC

When the thermosetting plastic is heated, links form between the polymers in the plastic. They become joined together into a permanent structure. The plastic is then left to cool. The thermoplastic does not need to be re-heated. It is simply left to solidify into the shape of the mould.

The strong links between the polymers of the thermosetting plastic mean that it holds its shape even at high temperatures. For this reason, plastics of this kind cannot be melted down and used again easily. The thermoplastic, however, has different types of links and can be melted down and used again.

MOULDING PLASTICS

If you think about the enormous range of objects made of plastic – thin sheets for wrapping food, long strips for curtain rails, hollow bottles and complicated toys – you will not be surprised that there are many different ways of moulding plastic. Some common ways of moulding or setting *thermoplastics* are shown below. The method chosen depends on the articles being made.

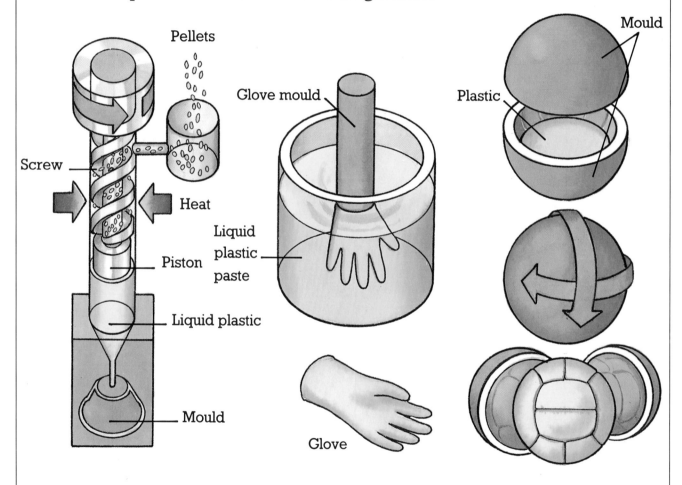

Granules of plastic are fed into a heated tube. A piston forces the liquid plastic down and out into a mould where it cools and hardens.

If a hollow, thin shape is being made, "dip moulding" may be the best method. Here a solid mould is dipped into a liquid plastic paste.

Beach balls are often made by "rotational casting". Raw plastic powder is fed into a mould and put in an oven. It melts in the mould.

Many *thermosetting* plastics have to be heated in order to mould them. This is called heat compression moulding. "Compression" means squeezing or squashing. The mould is usually made of steel and is held in a press in two pieces. Raw plastic is placed in the lower part of the mould and the two are then pressed together. The mould is heated up, the plastic softens and is squeezed into every part of the mould. It is left to harden in the press.

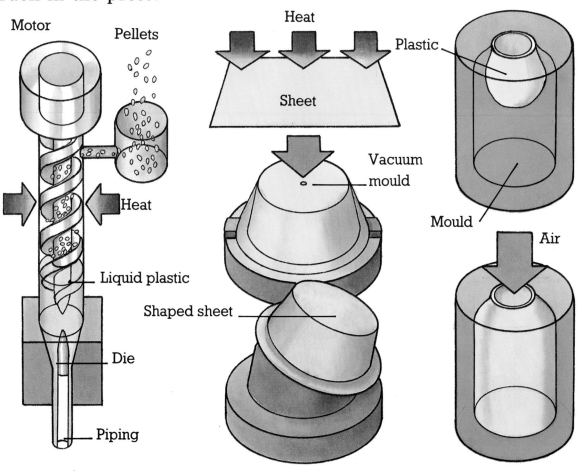

In "extrusion", molten thermoplastic is forced through a hole. The shape of the hole or "die" determines the article's shape.

A heated thermoplastic sheet can be shaped by "vacuum moulding". As air is drawn out, the sheet is sucked into the mould.

In "blow moulding", a thin tube of thermoplastic is extruded and sealed at one end. Air is blasted into the tube, forcing the plastic into the mould.

MAKING HARD SHEETS

Plastics are not always moulded into shapes – we often need sheets of plastic. Perspex is a type of thermosetting plastic which is excellent for making windows and roof lights. It is as clear as glass and does not break as easily. Liquid plastic is poured between two sheets of glass, sealed with rubber. The glass sheets are clamped tightly together and passed through a hot oven. The finished sheet, which is called Perspex, can then be removed.

Table tops and other surfaces are sometimes protected and decorated with sheets called "laminates". The best known laminate is called "formica". This is made up of layers of paper and plastic. It forms a very hard surface which is resistant to heat and does not stain.

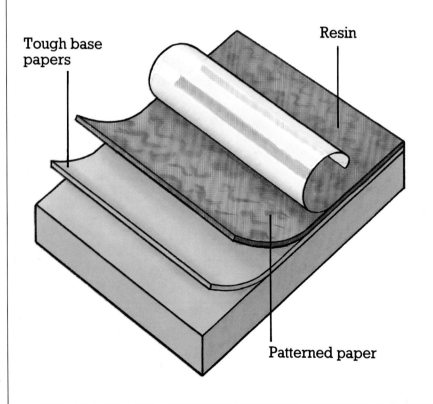

Tough base papers

Resin

Patterned paper

Formica is a hard sheet which is made up of three different layers of material. The inner layer is made of cheap brown paper containing Bakelite resin. This layer is then covered with white paper which has a pattern printed on it. This layer also contains colourless melamine resin. Finally, a plain, thin sheet of white paper containing more resin is placed on top. This layer is called the "overlay" and protects the pattern beneath it. Formica is a trade name.

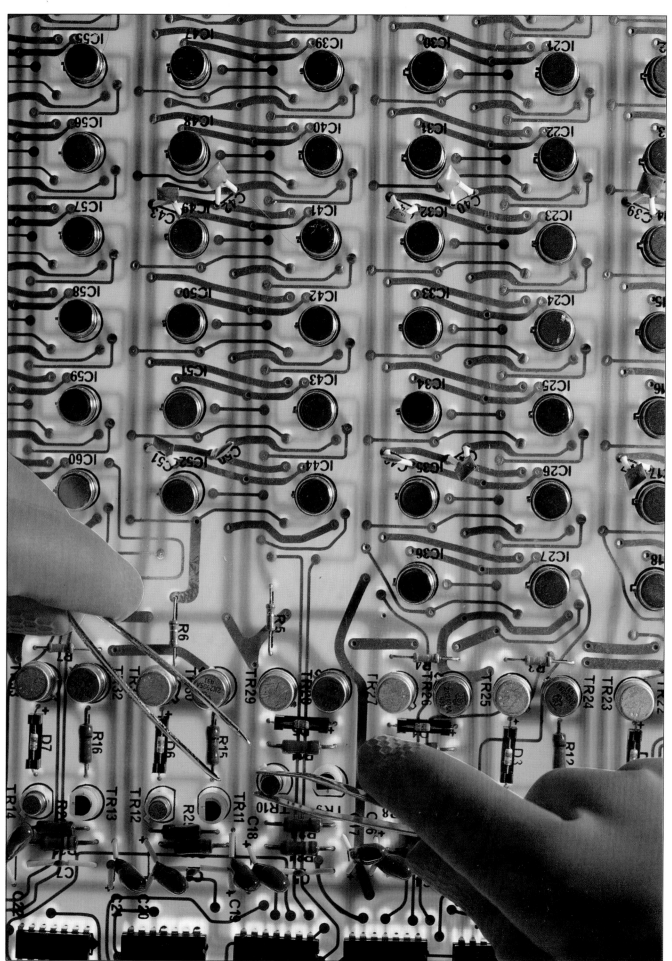

An electronic circuit board is mounted on a clear sheet of Perspex

MAKING FLEXIBLE SHEETS

Laminates and Perspex are both hard. Different plastics are needed to make flexible sheets. There are many uses for flexible sheets – carrier bags, light raincoats, shower curtains and food packaging are just a few examples.

Food and other articles are often "shrink wrapped". The first stage in shrink wrapping is to heat thin plastic film and stretch it. When it cools the film stays stretched. It is then wrapped around the article being packaged and sealed. The wrapped article is then passed through a hot tunnel which makes the plastic soft again. It then shrinks to its original size, wrapping the article very tightly.

Polythene sheets are usually made by a sort of extrusion. It is called the "tubular film process". Raw plastic pellets are heated and the molten plastic is forced through a tube. A jet of cold air is blown through the tube making it blow up like a balloon. The plastic is then stretched into thin sheets.

Plastic pellets

Heat

Polythene sheet

Circular slit

Rainwear is often made from flexible plastic or waterproofed with plastic

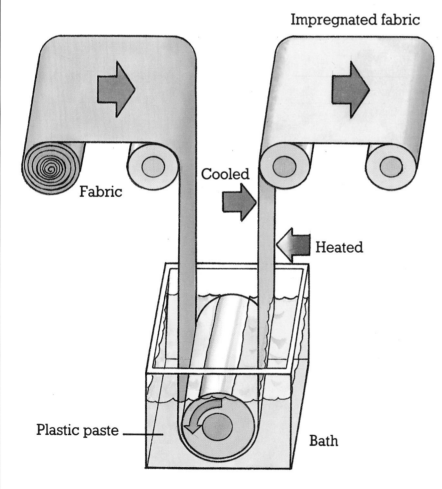

Impregnated fabric

Fabric

Cooled

Heated

Plastic paste

Bath

It is possible to make fabrics waterproof by soaking or "impregnating" them with plastic. The fabric is wound round a roller which is in a bath of plastic paste. The plastic soaks into the fabric. As it is wound out of the bath it is first heated and then cooled. The plastic is now set and the fabric is wound onto rollers ready to be made up into waterproof garments such as raincoats, or for use in tent making. Or the fabrics may be coated with plastic on one side. This process is called "calendering" and is also used for waterproofing.

PAINTS AND ADHESIVES

Did you know that paints and adhesives contain plastics? Many kinds of paint are made up of three different chemicals. One is the "pigment" which provides the colour; one is the plastic which holds the pigment in place and gives a shiny finish; and the third is a "solvent", usually white spirit, which makes the paint runny and easy to use. When the solvent evaporates, only the pigment and plastic are left. The paint is now dry. Paints used for decorating houses dry naturally, but cars are sprayed with paint which has to be dried in an oven.

Strong glues are made of thermosetting plastics called epoxy resins. They can stick metal, glass, china, wood – in fact almost anything!

Glues made from thermosetting plastics can set without heating

Some paints contain plastic to bind the pigment

FOAMS

Bubbles can be put into plastics to turn them into foams. Plastic foams have a number of uses. They are excellent materials for insulating, packaging and for making soft furnishings.

Flexible foam is used to make cushions and mattresses. Thin sheets of flexible foam are sometimes used to line clothes to make them warmer. Artificial sponges, draught excluders and paint rollers can all be made from this type of foam. Rigid foam is mainly used as a heat insulator. It is injected into the spaces between the outer walls of houses to keep them warmer. Polystyrene, a rigid foam, is also used for packaging.

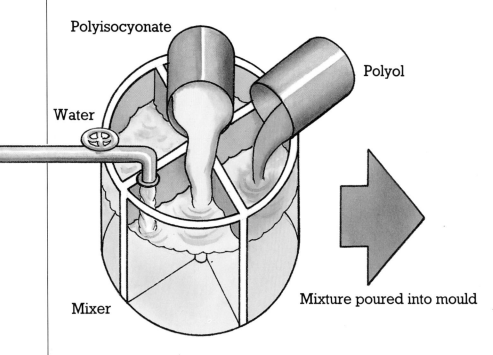

Polyisocyonate

Polyol

Water

Mixer

Mixture poured into mould

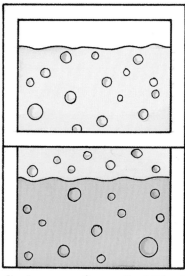

Carbon gas forms 'bubbles'

Rigid foams are made from thermosetting plastics, such as polyurethane. Liquid polyurethane is mixed very hard with an acid and a foaming agent. The mixture froths and sets almost immediately into a lightweight, rigid foam. Polyisocyonate and Polyol are the two basic materials which react together to make polyurethane. The reaction creates enough gas to make foam right away. Polyurethane is used as insulation.

Stacks of chairs made from polystyrene and flexible foam

SYNTHETIC FIBRES

Plastics are even used to make synthetic fabrics for clothes, curtains, sheets and carpets. Nylon, polyester and acrylic are all plastic fabrics. They are made from thermoplastics. You may wonder why it is necessary to make synthetic fabrics when there are natural ones, like cotton and wool. The answer is that natural fabrics are expensive and in short supply. Clothes made from synthetic fabrics have some advantages too – they do not crease much and they do not shrink in the wash. However, they are not so comfortable to wear, or as warm, as natural fabrics. Synthetic fabrics are often mixed with natural ones to combine the advantages of both.

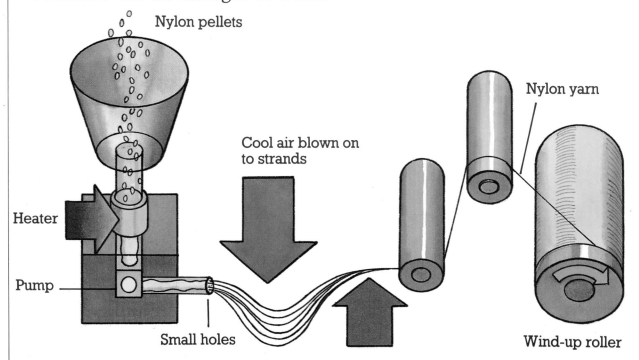

The long threads, or "fibres", used to make synthetic fabrics are made by extrusion. The diagram shows nylon fibres being made by a process called "melt spinning".

The plastic pellets are melted and forced through very fine holes in a machine called a "spinneret". The fibres harden as they cool and are wound onto a roller, ready to be woven.

Synthetic fibres are wound onto reels ready for weaving

RECYCLING

We throw millions of tonnes of plastics into our dustbins every year. Most of this is buried in refuse sites along with our other rubbish. But, unlike wood or metals, plastics will remain there more or less forever as they do not rot. This means that plastic rubbish remains unsightly. It also means that our valuable resources of oil are being wasted. But there are ways of reducing this wastage. Some plastics have been made which are "biodegradable". This means they will break down naturally in the soil. Other plastics could be recycled. Thermoplastics could be melted down and re-used. Some plastics can be burned and used as a fuel to provide heat and power.

Piles of rubbish – paper rots but plastic is there to stay

Plastic waste can be a wildlife hazard – the inset shows a recycling centre

THE STORY OF A PLASTIC TOY

1. OIL OR GAS IS PUMPED OUT OF THE EARTH AND IS SENT TO THE REFINERY.
2. IT IS THEN REFINED INTO DIFFERENT CHEMICALS FROM WHICH PLASTICS ARE MADE.

7. THE VARIOUS PARTS ARE MOULDED BY INJECTION MOULDING AND ARE THEN SENT TO THE TOY FACTORY 8.

3. THE PLASTIC TOY IS FIRST DESIGNED AND A MODEL IS MADE.
4. THE PACKAGING FOR THE TOY IS DESIGNED USING PAPER AND PLASTIC.
5. ONCE THE FINAL DESIGN IS APPROVED THE VARIOUS PARTS ARE SCULPTURED IN AND SENT OFF FOR MOULDS TO BE CAST IN METAL **6.**

MANY THOUSANDS CAN BE MADE THIS WAY AND CAN END UP IN SHOPS ALL OVER THE WORLD.

9. THE TOYS ARE PUT TOGETHER ON A FACTORY LINE WHERE EACH PERSON ADDS A BIT UNTIL IT IS COMPLETE. IT IS THEN PUT IN ITS PACKAGE READY TO BE DELIVERED TO THE SHOPS.

FACT FILE 1

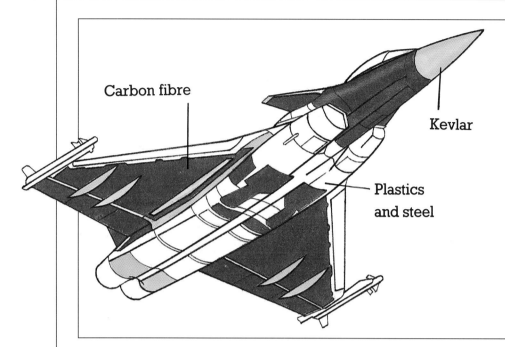

Carbon fibre

Kevlar

Plastics and steel

Plastics are not only used inside aircraft as trimmings – they also have an important part to play in the structure of advanced aircraft. Plastics are cheaper and lighter than metals and can be just as strong. So they are used in making the tail and the wings. Plastic glues are used to join sections of the plane.

Plastics have become a vital part of everyday life. This picture shows just some of the ways that a family might use plastics. Notice how plastics are used as hard and flexible sheets, as paints, foams and fabrics as well as moulded objects. Other materials could often be used instead. But plastics are light, cheap and may last longer. Use the information in this book to help you work out how each object might have been made. Turn over to see how the picture would change if plastics suddenly disappeared!

Insulating foam   Lightcover   Draining rack   Cat bowl   Formica top

Plant pot   Perspex greenhouse   Cups and tray   Dustbin

Bin bags

THE NAMES OF PLASTICS

Many plastics have long names which seem complicated at first. But the names often tell you what the plastic is made of. Once you understand how plastics get their names you will find them much easier to remember.

Plastics are made up of long chains called "polymers". The word polymer means "many parts". And that is a good description of a polymer as each one is made up of lots of smaller molecules. For example, polyethene is a common plastic. It is made of polymers containing lots of ethene molecules. The name polyethene, or polythene for short, describes what the plastic is made of. In the same way, polystyrene is made of lots of styrene molecules. Other plastics have shorter names which are trade names – they do not tell you anything about the plastic. Perspex and Orlon are examples of plastics known by their trade names.

Drain pipe   Helmet   Polyester shirt   Bucket   Safety glass   Torch (rubber)

Clothes peg   Hose pipe   Football   Rubber tyres   Soap suds   Paint

Foam interior

Many of the everyday things we use are made from plastic . . .

FACT FILE 2

We have seen how plastics are made from crude oil. They can also be made from coal and natural gas. But all three of these valuable resources have taken millions of years to form. Oil is the resource used most in the manufacture of plastics. But the world's oil supplies are being used up very quickly and our coal and gas will not last forever either. In fact oil reserves in the North Sea are expected to run low early in the next century. Oil will become too expensive to burn. So it is very important that we find alternative energy sources so that coal, oil and gas are still cheap enough to make into plastics.

Plastics have only been available in recent years – before the Second World War other materials were used instead. Some of these are shown opposite – in fact many of them are still used today and may be used again in greater quantities in the future. They have similar properties to some plastics but, at least at the moment, they are more expensive to mass-produce.

It has recently been discovered that plastics can be manufactured from wood. Perhaps this is not so surprising since coal is formed from dead, fossilised wood. So many of the chemicals found in coal are also found in wood. The advantage of using wood is that it can be replaced in a much shorter time. However, providing trees for plastics manufacture would take careful planning since large areas of the world are already short of trees which have been cut down to provide timber and paper. One important contribution to the problem which everyone can make is to use less plastic and throw less away.

Imagine life without plastics and see how we depend on this resource

Rubber

Rubber is collected as a liquid from the bark of rubber trees. 60% is used to make tyres.

Cellulose

Cellulose is found in plants. It can be used to make cellophane, rayon, paints and varnishes.

Horn

Horn is found in animal horns and nails. It can be split into sheets and used like glass or moulded.

Casein

This protein comes from milk. It can be used to made fibres of Lanital and Fibrolane.

Rayon

Rayon is a fibre made from cellulose. It is used in huge quantities to make car tyres and clothes.

Resin

Hard resins, such as amber, are fossils. Resins can also be got from living trees and used as varnish.

Glass

Glass is made from sand, soda ash and limestone. It is widely used for windows and bottles.

Gutta percha

This tree is a source of rubber used inside golf balls and was used to insulate electric wires.

Shellac

Lac insect larvae feed on tree sap and produce resin called shellac. It is used as a hard varnish.

GLOSSARY

Catalyst
A chemical which helps a chemical reaction take place more easily.

Cracking
The process of breaking and re-shaping molecules by heating with catalyst.

Die
A type of mould which can be used again.

Inflammable
Capable of burning easily.

Mould
A hollow structure in which molten or soft material is allowed to harden.

Pigment
A substance which is added to give things colour. Some pigments can colour things right through.

Raw plastics
Material which has not yet completed the process of becoming a plastic object.

Resins
Substances which come from the sap of some trees and other plants. Synthetic resin is a type of plastic.

Solvent
A substance, usually a liquid, which is able to dissolve other substances.

INDEX

PRINTED IN BELGIUM BY
proost
INTERNATIONAL BOOK PRODUCTION